**SCHOLASTIC**

# Solve-the-Riddle
# Math Practice
## Addition & Subtraction

**LIANE B. ONISH**

New York • Toronto • London • Auckland • Sydney
Mexico City • New Delhi • Hong Kong • Buenos Aires

**Teaching** *Resources*

# Hi, Mom!

Cover design by Ka-Yeon Kim-Li
Interior design by Holly Grundon
Interior illustrations by Anne Kennedy

ISBN-13: 978-0-545-16325-5
ISBN-10: 0-545-16325-0

# Contents

## About This Book

R esearch shows that to master math skills, students need lots of sustained practice. Quick recall of addition and subtraction facts and practice in regrouping are essential foundation skills for success in math. The silly riddles on the activity pages in this book will motivate students to complete the math problems and get this needed practice. Each answer is keyed to a letter. Located below the math problems is the solution to the riddle. Students write the letter that corresponds to each numerical answer to spell out the solution to the riddle. Voila! Math practiced, riddle solved!

## Meeting the Math Standards

The National Council of Teachers of Mathematics (NCTM) has outlined learning expectations and focal points–key concepts and skills for emphasis at different grade levels. The activities in this book align with the Number and Operations standards and curriculum focal points for grades 2 and 3 (nctm.org/standards).

For an overview of specific math skills covered in this book, see the Contents page. (These math skills are also listed at the top of each activity sheet.) Activity pages 5-29 (Riddles 1-25) focus on addition, pages 30-53 (Riddles 26-49) focus on subtraction, and pages 54-61 (Riddles 50-57) provide mixed addition and subtraction practice. Use your students' different ability levels as a guide when assigning the practice pages.

## Introducing the Activities

Read the riddle and math directions with students. Point out the letter below each answer's write-on line. Explain that the answers have the letters students will use to solve the riddle. After they complete the math, direct them to the bottom of the page. Have them read the number under the solution's first write-on line, then find that number in their math answers. Instruct them to write the letter that goes with that number answer on the line. When all of the letters have been filled in, invite students to reread the riddle and the solution. Discuss the word play used in the riddles, which rely mostly on multiple meanings and puns.

## Extra Practice Challenge

Invite students to create their own addition, subtraction, or mixed practice pages for their favorite riddles. Remind them that for twelve problems, the answer to the riddle can use no more than twelve different letters of the alphabet. Have students write a letter below the answer for each problem. Then have them check their work and write an answer key on a separate sheet of paper. Collect the student-made activity pages, mix them up, and distribute randomly.

### Math Vocabulary Teaching Tip

Review math vocabulary with students for terms such as: *add, plus, sum, total, subtract, minus, difference, ones, tens, hundreds,* and *regroup.* This is especially helpful for English language learners.

Name: _____    Date: _____

## Riddle 1

# What do frogs eat with their hamburgers?

Add.
Solve the riddle using your answers below.

| $\begin{array}{r} 11 \\ +\ 1 \\ \hline \text{A} \end{array}$ | $\begin{array}{r} 9 \\ +\ 4 \\ \hline \text{F} \end{array}$ | $\begin{array}{r} 14 \\ +\ 3 \\ \hline \text{T} \end{array}$ | $\begin{array}{r} 6 \\ +\ 5 \\ \hline \text{R} \end{array}$ | $\begin{array}{r} 10 \\ +\ 6 \\ \hline \text{S} \end{array}$ | $\begin{array}{r} 9 \\ +\ 1 \\ \hline \text{C} \end{array}$ |
| --- | --- | --- | --- | --- | --- |
| $\begin{array}{r} 14 \\ +\ 4 \\ \hline \text{H} \end{array}$ | $\begin{array}{r} 7 \\ +\ 2 \\ \hline \text{I} \end{array}$ | $\begin{array}{r} 8 \\ +\ 7 \\ \hline \text{N} \end{array}$ | $\begin{array}{r} 5 \\ +\ 3 \\ \hline \text{Y} \end{array}$ | $\begin{array}{r} 6 \\ +\ 8 \\ \hline \text{L} \end{array}$ | $\begin{array}{r} 4 \\ +\ 3 \\ \hline \text{E} \end{array}$ |

**Solve the Riddle!**   Write the letter that goes with each number.

___ ___ ___ ___ ___ ___
13  11  7  15  10  18

___ ___ ___ ___ ___
13  14  9  7  16

*Solve-the-Riddle Math Practice: Addition & Subtraction* © 2010 by Liane B. Onish. Scholastic Teaching Resources

Name: _____    Date: _____

## Riddle 2

# What is black and white and green?

Add.
Solve the riddle using your answers below.

| | | | | | |
|---|---|---|---|---|---|
| 2<br>12<br>+ 2<br>———<br>P | 9<br>4<br>+ 1<br>———<br>S | 10<br>6<br>+ 2<br>———<br>B | 2<br>4<br>+ 7<br>———<br>I | 5<br>6<br>+ 4<br>———<br>Z | 2<br>4<br>+ 1<br>———<br>U |
| 2<br>3<br>+ 4<br>———<br>E | 4<br>4<br>+ 3<br>———<br>C | 2<br>11<br>+ 4<br>———<br>K | 5<br>4<br>+ 3<br>———<br>T | 3<br>1<br>+ 6<br>———<br>R | 4<br>3<br>+ 1<br>———<br>A |

**Solve the Riddle!**   Write the letter that goes with each number.

___ ___ ___ ___ ___ ___ ___ ___
 8   14   9   8   14  13  11  17

___ ___ ___ ___ ___
 15   9   18  10   8

Name: _____   Date: _____

## Riddle (3)

# What word has the most letters?

Add.
Solve the riddle using your answers below.

| 15<br>+ 10<br>―――<br>O | 63<br>+ 10<br>―――<br>M | 41<br>+ 10<br>―――<br>R | 36<br>+ 10<br>―――<br>X | 64<br>+ 10<br>―――<br>Y | 51<br>+ 10<br>―――<br>D |
|---|---|---|---|---|---|
| 28<br>+ 10<br>―――<br>F | 80<br>+ 10<br>―――<br>L | 79<br>+ 10<br>―――<br>A | 58<br>+ 10<br>―――<br>B | 47<br>+ 10<br>―――<br>N | 26<br>+ 10<br>―――<br>I |

**Solve the Riddle!**   Write the letter that goes with each number.

___  ___  ___  ___  ___  ___  ___
73   89   36   90   68   25   46

Name: _____     Date: _____

## Riddle 4

# How does a lion like his steak?

Add.
Solve the riddle using your answers below.

|  |  |  |  |  |  |
|---|---|---|---|---|---|
| 5<br>+ 5<br>―――<br>B | 7<br>+ 7<br>―――<br>E | 10<br>+ 10<br>―――<br>U | 6<br>+ 6<br>―――<br>N | 13<br>+ 13<br>―――<br>I | 15<br>+ 15<br>―――<br>L |
| 19<br>+ 19<br>―――<br>D | 25<br>+ 25<br>―――<br>O | 21<br>+ 21<br>―――<br>R | 9<br>+ 9<br>―――<br>F | 12<br>+ 12<br>―――<br>M | 8<br>+ 8<br>―――<br>A |

**Solve the Riddle!**   Write the letter that goes with each number.

__ __ __ __ __ __   __ __ __ __
24  14  38  26  20  24   42  50  16  42

Name: _____     Date: _____

## Riddle  5

# What candies do
# scientists like best?

Add.
Solve the riddle using your answers below.

| | | | | | |
|---|---|---|---|---|---|
| 42<br>+ 7<br>———<br>A | 33<br>+ 5<br>———<br>R | 10<br>+ 9<br>———<br>E | 12<br>+ 4<br>———<br>D | 25<br>+ 2<br>———<br>T | 14<br>+ 0<br>———<br>X |
| 46<br>+ 1<br>———<br>S | 24<br>+ 2<br>———<br>I | 32<br>+ 3<br>———<br>P | 41<br>+ 1<br>———<br>L | 21<br>+ 8<br>———<br>M | 36<br>+ 1<br>———<br>N |

**Solve the Riddle!**   Write the letter that goes with each number.

$$-$$

___  ___  ___  ___  ___  ___     ___  ___  ___  ___  ___
19   14   35   19   38   26      29   26   37   27   47

Name: _____     Date: _____

## Riddle 6

# What does a teapot do when it is mad?

Add.
Solve the riddle using your answers below.

| 21<br>+ 14<br>———<br>N | 12<br>+ 15<br>———<br>I | 20<br>+ 19<br>———<br>U | 14<br>+ 14<br>———<br>W | 23<br>+ 31<br>———<br>P | 35<br>+ 13<br>———<br>T |
|---|---|---|---|---|---|
| 11<br>+ 31<br>———<br>L | 44<br>+ 12<br>———<br>S | 21<br>+ 43<br>———<br>B | 26<br>+ 21<br>———<br>R | 50<br>+ 18<br>———<br>O | 26<br>+ 53<br>———<br>E |

**Solve the Riddle!**   Write the letter that goes with each number.

___ ___   ___ ___ ___ ___ ___
27  48    64  42  68  28  56

___ ___ ___   ___ ___ ___ .
27  48  56    48  68  54

Name: _____  Date: _____

## Riddle 7

# What keeps mice from swimming?

Add.
Solve the riddle using your answers below.

| 20<br>+ 17<br>___<br>C | 18<br>+ 11<br>___<br>T | 32<br>+ 26<br>___<br>B | 13<br>+ 12<br>___<br>F | 26<br>+ 20<br>___<br>Y | 62<br>+ 21<br>___<br>S |
|---|---|---|---|---|---|
| 53<br>+ 10<br>___<br>H | 42<br>+ 12<br>___<br>D | 22<br>+ 70<br>___<br>I | 34<br>+ 41<br>___<br>E | 15<br>+ 23<br>___<br>P | 62<br>+ 35<br>___<br>A |

**Solve the Riddle!**   Write the letter that goes with each number.

___ ___ ___ ___ ___ ___ ___
37   97   29   25   92   83   63

Name: _____       Date: _____

## Riddle 8

# What do they use to clean the clouds?

Add.
Solve the riddle using your answers below.

| 18 <br> + 14 <br><br> ___ <br> P | 46 <br> + 32 <br><br> ___ <br> K | 39 <br> + 27 <br><br> ___ <br> N | 12 <br> + 13 <br><br> ___ <br> A | 17 <br> + 46 <br><br> ___ <br> T | 36 <br> + 18 <br><br> ___ <br> C |
|---|---|---|---|---|---|
| 16 <br> + 34 <br><br> ___ <br> R | 51 <br> + 33 <br><br> ___ <br> O | 23 <br> + 16 <br><br> ___ <br> Y | 36 <br> + 12 <br><br> ___ <br> E | 25 <br> + 46 <br><br> ___ <br> M | 46 <br> + 47 <br><br> ___ <br> S |

**Solve the Riddle!**   Write the letter that goes with each number.

___   ___   ___   ___   ___   ___   ___   ___   ___   ___   ___
93    78    39    93    54    50    25    32    48    50    93

**Riddle 9**

Name: _____   Date: _____

# What do you call a beach that keeps losing sand?

Add.
Solve the riddle using your answers below.

| 24<br>+ 19<br><br>___<br>S | 33<br>+ 27<br><br>___<br>E | 48<br>+ 39<br><br>___<br>B | 53<br>+ 18<br><br>___<br>O | 35<br>+ 59<br><br>___<br>N | 15<br>+ 37<br><br>___<br>D |
|---|---|---|---|---|---|
| 46<br>+ 38<br><br>___<br>R | 29<br>+ 46<br><br>___<br>U | 47<br>+ 49<br><br>___<br>L | 39<br>+ 24<br><br>___<br>H | 25<br>+ 47<br><br>___<br>A | 29<br>+ 19<br><br>___<br>I |

**Solve the Riddle!**   Write the letter that goes with each number.

___   ___ ___ ___ ___ ___
72     43   63   71   84   60

___   ___ ___ ___ ___
96     71   43   60   84

**13**

Name: _____    Date: _____

# Why didn't the astronauts on the moon stay longer?

Add.
Solve the riddle using your answers below.

| 47<br>+ 25<br><br>——<br>H | 22<br>+ 19<br><br>——<br>W | 17<br>+ 16<br><br>——<br>F | 57<br>+ 28<br><br>——<br>M | 29<br>+ 25<br><br>——<br>U | 38<br>+ 22<br><br>——<br>T |
|---|---|---|---|---|---|
| 19<br>+ 27<br><br>——<br>O | 35<br>+ 29<br><br>——<br>S | 47<br>+ 33<br><br>——<br>E | 59<br>+ 37<br><br>——<br>A | 49<br>+ 24<br><br>——<br>N | 18<br>+ 19<br><br>——<br>L |

## Solve the Riddle!   Write the letter that goes with each number.

___ ___ ___   ___ ___ ___ ___
60  72  80   85  46  46  73

___ ___ ___   ___ ___ ___ ___ .
41  96  64   33  54  37  37

Name: _____    Date: _____

## Riddle  11

# What do you get when you cross a pig and a centipede?

Add.
Solve the riddle using your answers below.

| 21<br>+ 39<br><br>___<br>N | 48<br>+ 26<br><br>___<br>M | 64<br>+ 18<br><br>___<br>L | 26<br>+ 27<br><br>___<br>A | 56<br>+ 36<br><br>___<br>R | 22<br>+ 19<br><br>___<br>B |
|---|---|---|---|---|---|
| 57<br>+ 18<br><br>___<br>C | 19<br>+ 24<br><br>___<br>G | 28<br>+ 38<br><br>___<br>D | 66<br>+ 24<br><br>___<br>S | 17<br>+ 64<br><br>___<br>O | 39<br>+ 19<br><br>___<br>E |

**Solve the Riddle!**   Write the letter that goes with each number.

___  ___  ___  ___  ___
41    53    75    81    60

___  ___  ___   ___  ___  ___  ___
53    60    66     82    58    43    90

Name: _____     Date: _____

## Riddle 12

# What happens once in every minute, twice in every moment, but not once in a hundred years?

Add.
Solve the riddle using your answers below.

| $\begin{array}{r}121\\+124\\\hline\end{array}$ | $\begin{array}{r}322\\+145\\\hline\end{array}$ | $\begin{array}{r}420\\+166\\\hline\end{array}$ | $\begin{array}{r}104\\+264\\\hline\end{array}$ | $\begin{array}{r}272\\+302\\\hline\end{array}$ | $\begin{array}{r}131\\+251\\\hline\end{array}$ |
|:---:|:---:|:---:|:---:|:---:|:---:|
| E | N | R | T | A | O |
| $\begin{array}{r}211\\+131\\\hline\end{array}$ | $\begin{array}{r}140\\+413\\\hline\end{array}$ | $\begin{array}{r}210\\+235\\\hline\end{array}$ | $\begin{array}{r}126\\+131\\\hline\end{array}$ | $\begin{array}{r}310\\+119\\\hline\end{array}$ | $\begin{array}{r}123\\+141\\\hline\end{array}$ |
| L | B | F | D | H | M |

**Solve the Riddle!**   Write the letter that goes with each number.

368    429    245

____  ____  ____  ____  ____  ____     ____
342   245   368   368   245   586     264

Name: _____    Date: _____

## Riddle 13

# What wobbles
# when it flies?

Add.
Solve the riddle using your answers below.

| 213<br>+135<br><br>___<br>L | 422<br>+210<br><br>___<br>M | 303<br>+102<br><br>___<br>P | 113<br>+114<br><br>___<br>J | 661<br>+204<br><br>___<br>R | 534<br>+122<br><br>___<br>Y |
|---|---|---|---|---|---|
| 319<br>+280<br><br>___<br>E | 243<br>+531<br><br>___<br>O | 730<br>+133<br><br>___<br>A | 110<br>+170<br><br>___<br>C | 823<br>+111<br><br>___<br>B | 101<br>+610<br><br>___<br>T |

**Solve the Riddle!**    Write the letter that goes with each number.

_

___  ___  ___  ___  ___  ___
863  227  599  348  348  656

___  ___  ___  ___  ___  ___
280  774  405  711  599  865

Name: _____     Date: _____

## Riddle 14

# What is a mermaid?

Add.
Solve the riddle using your answers below.

| 102<br>+315<br><br>E | 553<br>+216<br><br>C | 116<br>+241<br><br>A | 241<br>+403<br><br>R | 774<br>+122<br><br>D | 213<br>+312<br><br>F |
|---|---|---|---|---|---|
| 215<br>+714<br><br>B | 537<br>+261<br><br>H | 230<br>+102<br><br>P | 380<br>+500<br><br>I | 241<br>+432<br><br>S | 100<br>+301<br><br>L |

**Solve the Riddle!** Write the letter that goes with each number.

―

___  ___  ___  ___  ___  ___  ___  ___
357  896  417  417  332   673  798  417

___  ___  ___  ___
525  880  673  798

Name: _____        Date: _____

## Riddle 15

# What can you catch from the third letter of the alphabet?

Add.
Solve the riddle using your answers below.

| 113 +348 | 819 +138 | 574 +212 | 273 +317 | 371 +491 | 125 +320 |
|---|---|---|---|---|---|
| N | S | T | B | A | K |
| 203 +301 | 514 +306 | 100 +119 | 213 +418 | 572 +211 | 229 +139 |
| L | E | I | C | M | P |

**Solve the Riddle!**   Write the letter that goes with each number.

\_ \_\_ \_\_ \_\_ \_\_ \_\_ \_\_ \_\_ \_\_
631  957  219  631  445  461  820  957  957

Name: _____          Date: _____

## Riddle 16

# What part did the queen bee have in the rock band?

Add.
Solve the riddle using your answers below.

| 425<br>+282<br>‾‾‾‾<br>E | 177<br>+107<br>‾‾‾‾<br>H | 267<br>+642<br>‾‾‾‾<br>N | 401<br>+369<br>‾‾‾‾<br>A | 192<br>+463<br>‾‾‾‾<br>G | 489<br>+109<br>‾‾‾‾<br>L |
|---|---|---|---|---|---|
| 274<br>+171<br>‾‾‾‾<br>I | 353<br>+386<br>‾‾‾‾<br>T | 483<br>+132<br>‾‾‾‾<br>D | 142<br>+186<br>‾‾‾‾<br>B | 228<br>+291<br>‾‾‾‾<br>S | 509<br>+445<br>‾‾‾‾<br>R |

**Solve the Riddle!**   Write the letter that goes with each number.

___ ___ ___ ___
598  707  770  615

___ ___ ___ ___ ___ ___ ___
519  739  445  909  655  707  954

   *Solve-the-Riddle Math Practice: Addition & Subtraction* © 2010 by Liane B. Onish. Scholastic Teaching Resources

Name: _____     Date: _____

## Riddle  17

# Who cleans the fish's room?

Add.
Solve the riddle using your answers below.

| 217<br>+ 124<br><br>___<br>I | 128<br>+ 145<br><br>___<br>R | 229<br>+ 266<br><br>___<br>T | 193<br>+ 183<br><br>___<br>B | 279<br>+ 313<br><br>___<br>E | 138<br>+ 116<br><br>___<br>D |
|---|---|---|---|---|---|
| 144<br>+ 294<br><br>___<br>H | 182<br>+ 180<br><br>___<br>O | 260<br>+ 261<br><br>___<br>P | 126<br>+ 139<br><br>___<br>A | 284<br>+ 153<br><br>___<br>S | 392<br>+ 161<br><br>___<br>M |

**Solve the Riddle!**  Write the letter that goes with each number.

—

___ ___ ___   ___ ___ ___   ___ ___ ___ ___
495 438 592  553 592 273  553 265 341 254

Name: _____   Date: _____

# Waiter! What is this fly doing in my soup?

Add.
Solve the riddle using your answers below.

| 156 +624 | 530 +291 | 628 +319 | 282 +242 | 492 +141 | 224 +148 |
|:---:|:---:|:---:|:---:|:---:|:---:|
| C | N | E | O | R | A |
| 455 +235 | 282 +287 | 386 +332 | 265 +592 | 826 +159 | 242 +164 |
| B | H | T | S | K | F |

**Solve the Riddle!**   Write the letter that goes with each number.

____ ____ ____
718  569  947

____ ____ ____ ____ ____ ____ ____ ____ ____ ____ **?**
690  372  780  985  857  718  633  524  985  947

*Solve-the-Riddle Math Practice: Addition & Subtraction* © 2010 by Liane B. Onish. Scholastic Teaching Resources

Name: _____     Date: _____

## Riddle 19

# What do you call a tall pile of cats?

Add.
Solve the riddle using your answers below.

| 547<br>+274<br>———<br>———<br>R | 675<br>+117<br>———<br>———<br>W | 216<br>+448<br>———<br>———<br>V | 333<br>+187<br>———<br>———<br>P | 589<br>+356<br>———<br>———<br>A | 126<br>+317<br>———<br>———<br>T |
|---|---|---|---|---|---|
| 299<br>+437<br>———<br>———<br>M | 198<br>+183<br>———<br>———<br>H | 318<br>+139<br>———<br>———<br>E | 499<br>+176<br>———<br>———<br>N | 189<br>+129<br>———<br>———<br>O | 557<br>+405<br>———<br>———<br>I |

**Solve the Riddle!**   Write the letter that goes with each number.

—                              —
___   ___  ___  ___  ___      ___  ___  ___  ___  ___
945   736  457  318  792      675  443  945  962  675

Name: _____     Date: _____

## Riddle 20

# What dessert do fish serve at their parties?

Add.
Solve the riddle using your answers below.

| 574<br>+268<br>———<br>C | 176<br>+117<br>———<br>N | 478<br>+291<br>———<br>K | 279<br>+246<br>———<br>B | 317<br>+319<br>———<br>R | 574<br>+397<br>———<br>T |
|---|---|---|---|---|---|
| 318<br>+219<br>———<br>E | 179<br>+149<br>———<br>A | 285<br>+165<br>———<br>S | 416<br>+376<br>———<br>P | 195<br>+192<br>———<br>J | 236<br>+378<br>———<br>F |

**Solve the Riddle!**   Write the letter that goes with each number.

_____ _____ _____ _____   _____ _____ _____ _____ _____
842   636   328   525    842   328   769   537   450

*Solve-the-Riddle Math Practice: Addition & Subtraction* © 2010 by Liane B. Onish. Scholastic Teaching Resources

Name: _____ Date: _____

# Riddle 21

# What is a computer's favorite snack?

Add.
Solve the riddle using your answers below.

| 227<br>+285<br><br>___<br>O | 189<br>+266<br><br>___<br>C | 267<br>+346<br><br>___<br>B | 166<br>+168<br><br>___<br>A | 275<br>+245<br><br>___<br>P | 149<br>+179<br><br>___<br>M |
|---|---|---|---|---|---|
| 274<br>+129<br><br>___<br>I | 129<br>+186<br><br>___<br>H | 488<br>+139<br><br>___<br>L | 162<br>+189<br><br>___<br>S | 388<br>+149<br><br>___<br>R | 128<br>+288<br><br>___<br>N |

**Solve the Riddle!**  Write the letter that goes with each number.

___   ___   ___   ___   ___   –   ___   ___   ___   ___   ___
328   403   455   537   512      455   315   403   520   351

Name: _____    Date: _____

## Riddle 22

# What teeth cannot be trusted?

Add.
Solve the riddle using your answers below.

| 357<br>+266<br>——<br>T | 456<br>+354<br>——<br>U | 375<br>+187<br>——<br>R | 249<br>+195<br>——<br>F | 569<br>+134<br>——<br>N | 475<br>+436<br>——<br>L |
|---|---|---|---|---|---|
| 178<br>+197<br>——<br>A | 256<br>+276<br>——<br>B | 476<br>+179<br>——<br>E | 168<br>+659<br>——<br>I | 189<br>+147<br>——<br>H | 489<br>+299<br>——<br>S |

**Solve the Riddle!**  Write the letter that goes with each number.

___ ___ ___ ___ ___    ___ ___ ___ ___ ___
444  375  911  788  655    623  655  655  623  336

*Solve-the-Riddle Math Practice: Addition & Subtraction* © 2010 by Liane B. Onish. Scholastic Teaching Resources

## Riddle 23

Name: _____  Date: _____

# Who taught Superman to tell time?

Add.
Solve the riddle using your answers below.

| 168<br>+667<br>_____<br>R | 354<br>+289<br>_____<br>D | 267<br>+487<br>_____<br>K | 193<br>+299<br>_____<br>W | 494<br>+139<br>_____<br>E | 574<br>+346<br>_____<br>C |
|---|---|---|---|---|---|
| 187<br>+279<br>_____<br>N | 165<br>+146<br>_____<br>L | 378<br>+129<br>_____<br>U | 289<br>+689<br>_____<br>O | 498<br>+284<br>_____<br>T | 598<br>+223<br>_____<br>S |

**Solve the Riddle!**   Write the letter that goes with each number.

920  311  978  920  754    754  633  466  782

Name: _____     Date: _____

## Riddle 24

# Why did the queen say the pie was for the birds?

Regroup to add.
Solve the riddle using your answers below.

| 408<br>+237 | 507<br>+345 | 309<br>+478 | 201<br>+229 | 103<br>+658 | 607<br>+316 |
|:---:|:---:|:---:|:---:|:---:|:---:|
| ———<br>O | ———<br>M | ———<br>I | ———<br>A | ———<br>P | ———<br>T |
| 349<br>+209 | 139<br>+107 | 228<br>+104 | 317<br>+307 | 709<br>+106 | 167<br>+309 |
| ———<br>E | ———<br>H | ———<br>L | ———<br>S | ———<br>R | ———<br>W |

### Solve the Riddle!   Write the letter that goes with each number.

___ ___ ___ ___ ___
787  923  476  430  624

___ ___ ___  ___ ___ ___ ___ ___ .
923  645  645  923  476  558  558  923

Name: _____     Date: _____

# Riddle 25

## Who do ducks see when they are sick?

Add.
Solve the riddle using your answers below.

| 408<br>+125<br>___<br><br>U | 314<br>+306<br>___<br><br>Y | 107<br>+384<br>___<br><br>T | 558<br>+207<br>___<br><br>B | 608<br>+232<br>___<br><br>N | 505<br>+419<br>___<br><br>K |
|---|---|---|---|---|---|
| 268<br>+107<br>___<br><br>H | 409<br>+349<br>___<br><br>R | 406<br>+506<br>___<br><br>O | 107<br>+179<br>___<br><br>C | 239<br>+308<br>___<br><br>D | 406<br>+279<br>___<br><br>E |

**Solve the Riddle!**   Write the letter that goes with each number.

____  ____  ____   ____  ____  ____  ____   **–**   ____  ____  ____
491   375   685    547   533   286   924        491   912   758

Name: _____  Date: _____

## Riddle 26

# What do snowmen like to eat for breakfast?

Subtract.
Solve the riddle using your answers below.

| 17<br>− 1<br>——<br>P | 14<br>− 2<br>——<br>F | 18<br>− 3<br>——<br>A | 13<br>− 4<br>——<br>K | 18<br>− 0<br>——<br>S | 15<br>− 9<br>——<br>D |
|---|---|---|---|---|---|
| 15<br>− 4<br>——<br>O | 16<br>− 6<br>——<br>L | 18<br>− 1<br>——<br>R | 17<br>− 3<br>——<br>T | 16<br>− 8<br>——<br>H | 12<br>− 5<br>——<br>E |

**Solve the Riddle!**   Write the letter that goes with each number.

___ ___ ___ ___ ___ ___
12  17  11  18  14  7   6

___ ___ ___ ___ ___ ___
12  10  15  9   7   18

*Solve-the-Riddle Math Practice: Addition & Subtraction* © 2010 by Liane B. Onish. Scholastic Teaching Resources

Name: _____    Date: _____

## Riddle 27

# Why did the strawberry need to call a lawyer?

Subtract.
Solve the riddle using your answers below.

| 15<br>− 10<br>___<br>W | 73<br>− 10<br>___<br>J | 42<br>− 10<br>___<br>I | 86<br>− 10<br>___<br>E | 26<br>− 10<br>___<br>L | 51<br>− 10<br>___<br>S |
|---|---|---|---|---|---|
| 38<br>− 10<br>___<br>R | 60<br>− 10<br>___<br>A | 94<br>− 10<br>___<br>O | 78<br>− 10<br>___<br>M | 66<br>− 10<br>___<br>T | 47<br>− 10<br>___<br>N |

**Solve the Riddle!**    Write the letter that goes with each number.

___ ___    ___ ___ ___    ___ ___
32   56     5   50   41    32   37

___    ___ ___ ___ .
50     63   50   68

Name: _____  Date: _____

## Riddle 28

# What kind of dog likes to do the washing?

Subtract.
Solve the riddle using your answers below.

| | | | | | |
|---|---|---|---|---|---|
| 15<br>− 3<br>___<br>U | 18<br>− 5<br>___<br>M | 29<br>− 9<br>___<br>A | 37<br>− 1<br>___<br>E | 55<br>− 2<br>___<br>D | 44<br>− 4<br>___<br>V |
| 54<br>− 3<br>___<br>L | 24<br>− 2<br>___<br>N | 49<br>− 3<br>___<br>O | 37<br>− 2<br>___<br>R | 28<br>− 7<br>___<br>B | 39<br>− 5<br>___<br>T |

**Solve the Riddle!** Write the letter that goes with each number.

___ ___ ___ ___ ___ ___ ___ ___ −
20  51  20  12  22  53  35  46

___ ___ ___ ___
13  12  34  34

Name: _____    Date: _____

## Riddle 29

# What winter sport do toads like best?

Subtract.
Solve the riddle using your answers below.

| 96<br>− 12<br>___<br>P | 47<br>− 14<br>___<br>I | 29<br>− 18<br>___<br>N | 68<br>− 41<br>___<br>D | 55<br>− 35<br>___<br>O | 99<br>− 60<br>___<br>A |
|---|---|---|---|---|---|
| 39<br>− 21<br>___<br>H | 97<br>− 22<br>___<br>Y | 84<br>− 21<br>___<br>S | 76<br>− 24<br>___<br>C | 89<br>− 53<br>___<br>E | 58<br>− 13<br>___<br>R |

**Solve the Riddle!**   Write the letter that goes with each number.

___  ___  ___   ___  ___  ___  ___  ___
33   52   36    18   20   84   84   75

## Riddle 30

Name: _____ Date: _____

# Why did the snake check the tires on its car?

Subtract.
Solve the riddle using your answers below.

| 86 − 12 | 73 − 41 | 93 − 10 | 56 − 31 | 76 − 40 | 45 − 25 |
|---|---|---|---|---|---|
| A | V | H | L | E | B |
| 76 − 15 | 97 − 50 | 39 − 21 | 77 − 25 | 89 − 40 | 68 − 12 |
| T | R | I | D | O | S |

**Solve the Riddle!** Write the letter that goes with each number.

___ ___ ___ ___ ___ ___ ___
18  61   83  36  74  47  52

___ ___ ___ ___ ___ .
74  83  18  56  56

Name: _____     Date: _____

## Riddle 31

# How do witches break the sound barrier?

Subtract.
Solve the riddle using your answers below.

| 58<br>− 16<br>——<br>B | 47<br>− 42<br>——<br>W | 39<br>− 13<br>——<br>I | 96<br>− 83<br>——<br>T | 78<br>− 32<br>——<br>C | 99<br>− 49<br>——<br>O |
|---|---|---|---|---|---|
| 96<br>− 35<br>——<br>N | 88<br>− 34<br>——<br>M | 97<br>− 22<br>——<br>R | 25<br>− 24<br>——<br>K | 66<br>− 31<br>——<br>S | 26<br>− 10<br>——<br>H |

**Solve the Riddle!**   Write the letter that goes with each number.

___ ___ ___ ___   ___ ___ ___ ___ ___
5    26   13   16     35   50   61   26   46

___ ___ ___ ___ ___ ___
42   75   50   50   54   35

Name: _____    Date: _____

## Riddle 32

# Why is the octopus crossing the road?

Subtract.
Solve the riddle using your answers below.

| 86<br>− 32<br><br>E | 61<br>− 46<br><br>F | 63<br>− 29<br><br>T | 76<br>− 35<br><br>P | 94<br>− 56<br><br>K | 89<br>− 67<br><br>O |
|---|---|---|---|---|---|
| 96<br>− 69<br><br>G | 89<br>− 23<br><br>N | 64<br>− 14<br><br>R | 42<br>− 25<br><br>S | 86<br>− 11<br><br>I | 70<br>− 27<br><br>A |

**Solve the Riddle!**  Write the letter that goes with each number.

___ ___  ___ ___ ___  ___  ___ ___ ___
34  22   27  54  34   43   41  54  66

___ ___ ___  ___ ___ ___  ___ ___ ___
15  22  50   75  34  17   75  66  38

Name: _____     Date: _____

## Riddle  33

# What do you call a swimmer who was at the scene of a crime?

Subtract.
Solve the riddle using your answers below.

| | | | | | |
|---|---|---|---|---|---|
| 41<br>− 25<br>___<br>Y | 22<br>− 19<br>___<br>W | 74<br>− 16<br>___<br>F | 51<br>− 34<br>___<br>N | 62<br>− 29<br>___<br>U | 51<br>− 25<br>___<br>P |
| 71<br>− 23<br>___<br>O | 93<br>− 18<br>___<br>S | 53<br>− 29<br>___<br>E | 81<br>− 19<br>___<br>A | 37<br>− 28<br>___<br>T | 63<br>− 17<br>___<br>L |

**Solve the Riddle!**   Write the letter that goes with each number.

___  ___   ___  ___  ___
62   17    24   16   24

**-**

___  ___   ___   ___  ___  ___  ___
3    24    9     17   24   75   75

Name: _____    Date: _____

## Riddle 34

# What's the best way to communicate with fish?

Subtract.
Solve the riddle using your answers below.

| | | | | | |
|---|---|---|---|---|---|
| 52<br>− 23<br><br>___<br>O | 67<br>− 49<br><br>___<br>A | 73<br>− 17<br><br>___<br>D | 60<br>− 28<br><br>___<br>N | 51<br>− 37<br><br>___<br>E | 75<br>− 28<br><br>___<br>P |
| 90<br>− 29<br><br>___<br>I | 73<br>− 49<br><br>___<br>H | 62<br>− 27<br><br>___<br>M | 91<br>− 18<br><br>___<br>R | 98<br>− 29<br><br>___<br>L | 46<br>− 18<br><br>___<br>T |

**Solve the Riddle!**   Write the letter that goes with each number.

___ ___ ___ ___  ___ ___ ___ ___
56  73  29  47  28  24  14  35

___ ___ ___ ___ ___ .
18  69  61  32  14

*Solve-the-Riddle Math Practice: Addition & Subtraction* © 2010 by Liane B. Onish. Scholastic Teaching Resources

Name: _____   Date: _____

## Riddle 35

# How do you make a strawberry shake?

Subtract.
Solve the riddle using your answers below.

| 61<br>− 49<br>———<br>O | 77<br>− 49<br>———<br>D | 53<br>− 38<br>———<br>A | 94<br>− 48<br>———<br>R | 64<br>− 25<br>———<br>I | 72<br>− 14<br>———<br>K |
|---|---|---|---|---|---|
| 76<br>− 29<br>———<br>M | 95<br>− 86<br>———<br>T | 81<br>− 49<br>———<br>B | 92<br>− 18<br>———<br>E | 83<br>− 29<br>———<br>V | 91<br>− 28<br>———<br>H |

**Solve the Riddle!**   Write the letter that goes with each number.

__ __ __ __   __ __   __ __   __
9   15   58   74      39   9     9   12      15

__ __ __ __ __ __   __ __ __ __ __ .
63 12 46 46 12 46   47 12 54 39 74

Name: _____    Date: _____

## Riddle 36

# Why is this lion crossing the road?

Subtract.
Solve the riddle using your answers below.

| 424<br>− 121<br><br>___<br>E | 299<br>− 107<br><br>___<br>P | 576<br>− 130<br><br>___<br>R | 698<br>− 541<br><br>___<br>T | 379<br>− 101<br><br>___<br>A | 867<br>− 125<br><br>___<br>L |
|---|---|---|---|---|---|
| 445<br>− 234<br><br>___<br>N | 947<br>− 113<br><br>___<br>G | 878<br>− 242<br><br>___<br>O | 536<br>− 131<br><br>___<br>D | 787<br>− 207<br><br>___<br>I | 679<br>− 310<br><br>___<br>H |

## Solve the Riddle!  Write the letter that goes with each number.

___ ___  ___ ___ ___  ___ ___  ___ ___ ___
157  636  834  303  157  157  636  157  369  303

___ ___ ___ ___ ___  ___ ___ ___ ___ ___
636  157  369  303  446  192  446  580  405  303

Name: _____  Date: _____

## Riddle 37

# What do you call a flower shop that is burning down?

Subtract.
Solve the riddle using your answers below.

|  |  |  |  |  |  |
|---|---|---|---|---|---|
| 346<br>− 124<br><br>___<br>E | 452<br>− 121<br><br>___<br>T | 588<br>− 132<br><br>___<br>O | 498<br>− 194<br><br>___<br>A | 575<br>− 112<br><br>___<br>I | 499<br>− 217<br><br>___<br>N |
| 743<br>− 231<br><br>___<br>F | 406<br>− 203<br><br>___<br>C | 575<br>− 135<br><br>___<br>L | 676<br>− 131<br><br>___<br>P | 519<br>− 219<br><br>___<br>R | 693<br>− 131<br><br>___<br>S |

## Solve the Riddle!   Write the letter that goes with each number.

___   ___   ___   ___   ___   ___   ___   ___
304   512   440   456   300   463   562   331

___   ___   ___   ___
512   463   300   222

Name: _____     Date: _____

## Riddle 38

# Why did the runner put a net over her head?

Subtract.
Solve the riddle using your answers below.

| 645<br>– 142<br>———<br>A | 521<br>– 210<br>———<br>B | 858<br>– 424<br>———<br>Y | 986<br>– 144<br>———<br>O | 755<br>– 235<br>———<br>L | 699<br>– 431<br>———<br>H |
|---|---|---|---|---|---|
| 879<br>– 720<br>———<br>E | 986<br>– 303<br>———<br>T | 785<br>– 510<br>———<br>D | 769<br>– 311<br>———<br>R | 519<br>– 412<br>———<br>C | 938<br>– 212<br>———<br>I |

**Solve the Riddle!**   Write the letter that goes with each number.

683   842   107   503   683   107   268

268   159   458   311   458   159   503   683   268

Name: _____     Date: _____

## Riddle 39

# What do you call the
# Invisible Boy's mom and dad?

Subtract.
Solve the riddle using your answers below.

| 854<br>− 213 | 771<br>− 635 | 989<br>− 444 | 690<br>− 338 | 479<br>− 211 | 532<br>− 119 |
|:---:|:---:|:---:|:---:|:---:|:---:|
| N | P | H | T | W | R |
| 814<br>− 621 | 547<br>− 166 | 879<br>− 143 | 675<br>− 121 | 718<br>− 497 | 983<br>− 223 |
| F | I | E | S | M | A |

### Solve the Riddle!   Write the letter that goes with each number.

_____  _____  _____   _____  _____  _____  _____  _____      −
545    381    554     352    413    760    641    554

_____  _____  _____  _____  _____  _____  _____
136    760    413    736    641    352    554

Name: _____     Date: _____

# Riddle 40

## Can the king's son write script?

Subtract.
Solve the riddle using your answers below.

| 587<br>− 218<br>___<br>O | 616<br>− 446<br>___<br>R | 486<br>− 169<br>___<br>T | 365<br>− 172<br>___<br>H | 672<br>− 249<br>___<br>A | 344<br>− 182<br>___<br>P |
|---|---|---|---|---|---|
| 572<br>− 419<br>___<br>N | 483<br>− 192<br>___<br>E | 519<br>− 131<br>___<br>W | 329<br>− 178<br>___<br>C | 590<br>− 165<br>___<br>I | 657<br>− 329<br>___<br>D |

**Solve the Riddle!**   Write the letter that goes with each number.

___ ___ ,  ___ ___
153  369      193  291

___ ___ ___ ___ ___ ___ .
162  170  425  153  151  291

Name: _____   Date: _____

## Riddle 41

# What trees do fortune-tellers like best?

Subtract.
Solve the riddle using your answers below.

| 537<br>− 287<br><br>—<br>C | 874<br>− 168<br><br>—<br>M | 768<br>− 396<br><br>—<br>K | 619<br>− 196<br><br>—<br>B | 887<br>− 249<br><br>—<br>R | 994<br>− 177<br><br>—<br>T |
|---|---|---|---|---|---|
| 298<br>− 149<br><br>—<br>E | 949<br>− 369<br><br>—<br>A | 686<br>−418<br><br>—<br>S | 891<br>−476<br><br>—<br>P | 358<br>− 197<br><br>—<br>L | 939<br>− 375<br><br>—<br>F |

**Solve the Riddle!**   Write the letter that goes with each number.

___ ___ ___ ___   ___ ___ ___ ___ ___
415  580  161  706   817  638  149  149  268

*Solve-the-Riddle Math Practice: Addition & Subtraction* © 2010 by Liane B. Onish. Scholastic Teaching Resources

Name: _____ Date: _____

## Riddle 42

# What do you call lambs that fight on the ocean?

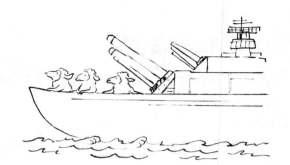

Subtract.
Solve the riddle using your answers below.

| 943<br>– 137<br><br>___<br>L | 551<br>– 227<br><br>___<br>N | 646<br>– 475<br><br>___<br>H | 767<br>– 218<br><br>___<br>R | 892<br>– 454<br><br>___<br>B | 565<br>– 295<br><br>___<br>U |
|---|---|---|---|---|---|
| 529<br>– 340<br><br>___<br>S | 958<br>– 191<br><br>___<br>A | 694<br>– 376<br><br>___<br>C | 829<br>– 177<br><br>___<br>T | 714<br>– 507<br><br>___<br>P | 824<br>– 261<br><br>___<br>E |

**Solve the Riddle!** Write the letter that goes with each number.

___ ___ ___ ___ ___ ___ —
438  767  652  652  806  563

___ ___ ___ ___ ___
189  171  563  563  207

Name: _____  Date: _____

# What did the trees say on the first day of spring?

Subtract.
Solve the riddle using your answers below.

| | | | | | |
|---|---|---|---|---|---|
| 952<br>− 234<br><br>―――<br>H | 721<br>− 346<br><br>―――<br>L | 868<br>− 529<br><br>―――<br>E | 562<br>− 459<br><br>―――<br>Y | 935<br>− 278<br><br>―――<br>W | 826<br>− 357<br><br>―――<br>N |
| 721<br>− 279<br><br>―――<br>S | 892<br>− 766<br><br>―――<br>A | 642<br>− 467<br><br>―――<br>C | 994<br>− 106<br><br>―――<br>F | 694<br>− 417<br><br>―――<br>T | 537<br>− 293<br><br>―――<br>R |

**Solve the Riddle!**   Write the letter that goes with each number.

___  ___  ___  ___   ___
657  718  126  277   126

‒

___  ___        ___  ___  ___  ___  !
244  339        375  339  126  888

Name: _____     Date: _____

## Riddle 44

# Which witch turns off the lights?

Subtract.
Solve the riddle using your answers below.

| | | | | | |
|---|---|---|---|---|---|
| 464<br>− 127<br><br>——<br>S | 748<br>− 239<br><br>——<br>I | 418<br>− 196<br><br>——<br>T | 687<br>− 159<br><br>——<br>C | 415<br>− 174<br><br>——<br>A | 386<br>− 189<br><br>——<br>H |
| 539<br>− 396<br><br>——<br>E | 913<br>− 147<br><br>——<br>K | 633<br>− 159<br><br>——<br>R | 977<br>− 219<br><br>——<br>L | 831<br>− 189<br><br>——<br>G | 423<br>− 238<br><br>——<br>W |

**Solve the Riddle!**   Write the letter that goes with each number.

___ ___ ___   ___ ___ ___ ___ ___ ___
222  197  143   758  509  642  197  222  337

___ ___ ___ ___ ___
185  509  222  528  197

## Riddle 45

Name: _____     Date: _____

# What does the wig say when he gets home?

Subtract.
Solve the riddle using your answers below.

| 532<br>– 134 | 642<br>– 379 | 423<br>– 238 | 731<br>– 257 | 653<br>– 397 | 913<br>– 266 |
|---|---|---|---|---|---|
| ___<br>O | ___<br>N | ___<br>E | ___<br>L | ___<br>D | ___<br>Y |
| 924<br>– 185 | 656<br>– 158 | 831<br>– 299 | 936<br>– 777 | 721<br>– 395 | 842<br>– 277 |
| ___<br>I | ___<br>A | ___<br>H | ___<br>M | ___<br>R | ___<br>U |

**Solve the Riddle!**   Write the letter that goes with each number.

___ ___  ___ ___ ___ ___ ___ ,
532  739   532  398  263  185  647

___ ___ ,  ___ ___ ___ ___ .
739  159   532  498  739  326

Name: _____    Date: _____

## Riddle 46

# What does a tree say when it doesn't know the answer?

Subtract.
Solve the riddle using your answers below.

| 414 − 125 | 712 − 256 | 847 − 278 | 321 − 194 | 832 − 187 | 942 − 189 |
|:---:|:---:|:---:|:---:|:---:|:---:|
| M | R | U | A | I | D |
| 813 − 247 | 931 − 183 | 626 − 439 | 731 − 359 | 721 − 263 | 562 − 287 |
| P | G | N | S | T | E |

**Solve the Riddle!**  Write the letter that goes with each number.

____ ____ ____ ' ____ ____ '
748  275  275   645  289

____ ____ ____ ____ ____ ____ ____ .
372  458  569  289  566  275  753

Name: _____    Date: _____

## Riddle 47

# If an egg floats down the Mississippi River, where does it come from?

MISSISSIPPI RIVER

Subtract.
Solve the riddle using your answers below.

| | | | | | |
|---|---|---|---|---|---|
| 521<br>− 128<br>———<br><br>K | 842<br>− 268<br>———<br><br>T | 754<br>− 289<br>———<br><br>E | 422<br>− 135<br>———<br><br>H | 952<br>− 296<br>———<br><br>R | 341<br>− 188<br>———<br><br>A |
| 931<br>− 186<br>———<br><br>S | 813<br>− 585<br>———<br><br>C | 925<br>− 248<br>———<br><br>M | 721<br>− 359<br>———<br><br>D | 812<br>− 289<br>———<br><br>I | 625<br>− 189<br>———<br><br>N |

**Solve the Riddle!**   Write the letter that goes with each number.

___  ___  ___  ___  ___  ___  ___  ___
153   228  287  523  228  393  465  436

Name: _____    Date: _____

## Riddle 48

# What do geese get when they are cold or scared?

Subtract.
Solve the riddle using your answers below.

| 901<br>− 169<br><br>_____<br>B | 303<br>− 116<br><br>_____<br>A | 605<br>− 237<br><br>_____<br>U | 802<br>− 384<br><br>_____<br>R | 905<br>− 739<br><br>_____<br>M | 602<br>− 259<br><br>_____<br>O |
|---|---|---|---|---|---|
| 908<br>− 229<br><br>_____<br>F | 707<br>− 459<br><br>_____<br>E | 805<br>− 338<br><br>_____<br>P | 406<br>− 178<br><br>_____<br>L | 701<br>− 127<br><br>_____<br>S | 904<br>− 146<br><br>_____<br>G |

**Solve the Riddle!**    Write the letter that goes with each number.

467   248   343   467   228   248

732   368   166   467   574

Name: _____    Date: _____

## Riddle 49

# What advice can you get from your hands?

Subtract.
Solve the riddle using your answers below.

| 608<br>− 269<br><br>———<br>E | 703<br>− 528<br><br>———<br>F | 580<br>− 357<br><br>———<br>A | 880<br>− 269<br><br>———<br>L | 402<br>− 194<br><br>———<br>P | 870<br>− 258<br><br>———<br>I |
|---|---|---|---|---|---|
| 902<br>− 138<br><br>———<br>T | 670<br>− 114<br><br>———<br>N | 703<br>− 269<br><br>———<br>B | 901<br>− 328<br><br>———<br>G | 506<br>− 157<br><br>———<br>S | 903<br>−796<br><br>———<br>R |

**Solve the Riddle!**    Write the letter that goes with each number.

——  ——  ——  ——  ——  ——
175   612   556   573   339   107

——  ——  ——  ——
764   612   208   349

Name: _____ Date: _____

## Riddle 50

# What do you say to a farmer who wants to talk about corn?

Add or subtract.
Solve the riddle using your answers below.

| | | | | | |
|---|---|---|---|---|---|
| 5<br>+ 6<br>——<br>M | 11<br>− 6<br>——<br>I | 10<br>+ 5<br>——<br>D | 16<br>− 8<br>——<br>L | 13<br>− 4<br>——<br>C | 7<br>+ 6<br>——<br>F |
| 17<br>− 0<br>——<br>R | 14<br>+ 2<br>——<br>J | 18<br>− 4<br>——<br>A | 7<br>+ 3<br>——<br>N | 9<br>+ 9<br>——<br>S | 17<br>− 5<br>——<br>E |

**Solve the Riddle!** Write the letter that goes with each number.

___ ___ ' ___ ___ ___   ___ ___ ___ ___ .
  5   11     14   8   8     12   14   17   18

Name: _____     Date: _____

## Riddle 51

# What did the mitten tell the thumb?

Add or subtract.
Solve the riddle using your answers below.

| 34<br>+ 14<br>___<br><br>L | 17<br>+ 5<br>___<br><br>C | 29<br>− 18<br>___<br><br>V | 44<br>− 19<br>___<br><br>N | 45<br>− 4<br>___<br><br>A | 37<br>+ 17<br>___<br><br>E |
|---|---|---|---|---|---|
| 41<br>− 2<br>___<br><br>I | 37<br>− 30<br>___<br><br>O | 38<br>+ 29<br>___<br><br>U | 42<br>+ 14<br>___<br><br>G | 24<br>− 19<br>___<br><br>Y | 39<br>− 5<br>___<br><br>R |

**Solve the Riddle!**   Write the letter that goes with each number.

___ ___ ___ ___ ___ ___   ___ ___ ___ .
39   56   48   7   11   54     5   7   67

Name: _____     Date: _____

## Riddle 52

# What male bug can float?

Add or subtract.
Solve the riddle using your answers below.

| 46<br>+43<br>⎯⎯<br>U | 75<br>− 66<br>⎯⎯<br>E | 17<br>+ 36<br>⎯⎯<br>N | 49<br>+ 18<br>⎯⎯<br>B | 75<br>− 59<br>⎯⎯<br>G | 54<br>− 23<br>⎯⎯<br>O |
|---|---|---|---|---|---|
| 99<br>− 29<br>⎯⎯<br>A | 61<br>+ 31<br>⎯⎯<br>R | 26<br>− 19<br>⎯⎯<br>S | 17<br>+ 11<br>⎯⎯<br>Y | 53<br>+ 29<br>⎯⎯<br>H | 97<br>− 53<br>⎯⎯<br>T |

**Solve the Riddle!**   Write the letter that goes with each number.

___ ___ ___ ___ ___  -  ___ ___ ___
70   67  31  89  28      70  53  44

**Riddle** 53

Name: _____  Date: _____

# What kitchen tool do knights fear most?

Add or subtract.
Solve the riddle using your answers below.

| | | | | | |
|---|---|---|---|---|---|
| 59<br>− 23<br>_____<br>A | 73<br>− 56<br>_____<br>R | 92<br>− 47<br>_____<br>H | 48<br>+ 21<br>_____<br>L | 14<br>+ 39<br>_____<br>C | 49<br>− 38<br>_____<br>O |
| 97<br>− 11<br>_____<br>T | 10<br>+ 42<br>_____<br>P | 59<br>+ 38<br>_____<br>N | 85<br>− 45<br>_____<br>D | 93<br>− 19<br>_____<br>S | 29<br>+ 59<br>_____<br>E |

**Solve the Riddle!**  Write the letter that goes with each number.

___ ___ ___   ___ ___ ___
86  45  88   53  36  97

___ ___ ___ ___ ___ ___
11  52  88  97  88  17

Name: _____     Date: _____

## Riddle 54

# Who had the first mobile home?

Add or subtract.
Solve the riddle using your answers below.

| 567<br>+ 132<br>_____<br>T | 216<br>+ 327<br>_____<br>L | 853<br>− 627<br>_____<br>U | 482<br>− 352<br>_____<br>F | 246<br>+ 725<br>_____<br>A | 694<br>− 491<br>_____<br>E |
|---|---|---|---|---|---|
| 796<br>− 228<br>_____<br>K | 651<br>+ 134<br>_____<br>N | 892<br>− 536<br>_____<br>R | 323<br>+ 224<br>_____<br>O | 986<br>− 132<br>_____<br>H | 343<br>+ 139<br>_____<br>D |

**Solve the Riddle!**   Write the letter that goes with each number.

___ ___ ___   ___ ___ ___ ___ ___ ___
699 854 203   699 226 356 699 543 203

Name: _____    Date: _____

## Riddle 55

# What do you get when you cross an artist with a slob?

Add or subtract.
Solve the riddle using your answers below.

| 353<br>− 125 | 886<br>− 697 | 678<br>+ 267 | 171<br>+ 196 | 989<br>− 517 | 122<br>+ 688 |
|:---:|:---:|:---:|:---:|:---:|:---:|
| E | P | N | A | C | R |
| 138<br>+ 433 | 556<br>+ 183 | 963<br>− 166 | 219<br>+ 585 | 781<br>− 123 | 932<br>− 469 |
| M | O | K | T | I | S |

**Solve the Riddle!**   Write the letter that goes with each number.

___ ___ ___ ___ ___  **–**  ___ ___ ___ ___ ___ ___ ___ ___
367  571  228  463  463     804  228  810  189  658  228  472  228

Name: _____    Date: _____

## Riddle 56

# What game do little monsters like to play?

Add or subtract.
Solve the riddle using your answers below.

| 748<br>−437<br><br>___<br>F | 574<br>−419<br><br>___<br>E | 133<br>+129<br><br>___<br>S | 317<br>+487<br><br>___<br>T | 738<br>−218<br><br>___<br>I | 629<br>+298<br><br>___<br>N |
|---|---|---|---|---|---|
| 937<br>−248<br><br>___<br>A | 323<br>+413<br><br>___<br>H | 754<br>−276<br><br>___<br>K | 585<br>+279<br><br>___<br>D | 354<br>−257<br><br>___<br>R | 141<br>+102<br><br>___<br>M |

**Solve the Riddle!**   Write the letter that goes with each number.

___ ___ ___ ___   ___ ___ ___
736  520  864  155   689  927  864

___ ___ ___ ___ ___ ___
262  736  97  520  155  478

**Riddle 57**

Name: _____     Date: _____

# What did General George Washington say to his men before crossing the Delaware River?

Add or subtract.
Solve the riddle using your answers below.

|  |  |  |  |  |  |
|---|---|---|---|---|---|
| 408<br>+237<br><br>___<br>E | 503<br>− 345<br><br>___<br>H | 309<br>+478<br><br>___<br>N | 509<br>− 129<br><br>___<br>A | 103<br>+658<br><br>___<br>G | 604<br>− 319<br><br>___<br>L |
| 406<br>− 249<br><br>___<br>I | 302<br>− 134<br><br>___<br>T | 228<br>+ 104<br><br>___<br>B | 317<br>+ 307<br><br>___<br>D | 709<br>− 156<br><br>___<br>O | 167<br>+ 309<br><br>___<br>M |

**Solve the Riddle!**   Write the letter that goes with each number.

___ ___ ___ !   ___ ___ ___   ___ ___
476  645  787     761  645  168   157  787

___ ___ ___   ___ ___ ___ ___ !
168  158  645   332  553  380  168

# Answer Key

page 5: **Riddle 1**
*french flies*
A-12, F-13, T-17, R-11, S-16, C-10, H-18, I-9, N-15, Y-8, L-14, E-7

page 6: **Riddle 2**
*a seasick zebra*
P-16, S-14, B-18, I-13, Z-15, U-7, E-9, C-11, K-17, T-12, R-10, A-8

page 7: **Riddle 3**
*mailbox*
O-25, M-73, R-51, X-46, Y-74, D-61, F-38, L-90, A-89, B-68, N-57, I-36

page 8: **Riddle 4**
*medium roar*
B-10, E-14, U-20, N-12, I-26, L-30, D-38, O-50, R-42, F-18, M-24, A-16

page 9: **Riddle 5**
*experi-mints*
A-49, R-38, E-19, D-16, T-27, X-14, S-47, I-26, P-35, L-42, M-29, N-37

page 10: **Riddle 6**
*It blows its top.*
N-35, I-27, U-39, W-28, P-54, T-48, L-42, S-56, B-64, R-47, O-68, E-79

page 11: **Riddle 7**
*catfish*
C-37, T-29, B-58, F-25, Y-46, S-83, H-63, D-54, I-92, E-75, P-38, A-97

page 12: **Riddle 8**
*skyscrapers*
P-32, K-78, N-66, A-25, T-63, C-54, R-50, O-84, Y-39, E-48, M-71, S-93

page 13: **Riddle 9**
*a shore loser*
S-43, E-60, B-87, O-71, N-94, D-52, R-84, U-75, L-96, H-63, A-72, I-48

page 14: **Riddle 10**
*The moon was full.*
H-72, W-41, F-33, M-85, U-54, T-60, O-46, S-64, E-80, A-96, N-73, L-37

page 15: **Riddle 11**
*bacon and legs*
N-60, M-74, L-82, A-53, R-92, B-41, C-75, G-43, D-66, S-90, O-81, E-58

page 16: **Riddle 12**
*the letter m*
E-245, N-467, R-586, T-368, A-574, O-382, L-342, B-553, F-445, D-257, H-429, M-264

page 17: **Riddle 13**
*a jelly-copter*
L-348, N-632, P-405, J-227, R-865, Y-656, E-599, O-774, A-863, C-280, B-934, T-711

page 18: **Riddle 14**
*a deep-she fish*
E-417, C-769, A-357, R-644, D-896, F-525, B-929, H-798, P-332, I-880, S-673, L-401

page 19: **Riddle 15**
*c-sickness*
N-461, S-957, T-786, B-590, A-862, K-445, L-504, E-820, I-219, C-631, M-783, P-368

page 20 **riddle 16**
*lead stinger*
E-707, H-284, N-909, A-770, G-655, L-598, I-445, T-739, D-615, B-328, S-519, R-954

page 21: **Riddle 17**
*the mer-maid*
I-341, R-273, T-495, B-376, E-592, D-254, H-438, O-362, P-521, A-265, S-437, M-553

page 22 **Riddle 18**
*The backstroke?*
C-780, N-821, E-947, O-524, R-633, A-372, B-690, H-569, T-718, S-857, K-985, F-406

page 23: **Riddle 19**
*a meow-ntain*
R-821, W-792, V-664, P-520, A-945, T-443, M-736, H-381, E-457, N-675, O-318, I-962

page 24: **Riddle 20**

*crab cakes*

C-842, N-293, K-769, B-525, R-636, T-971, E-537, A-328, S-450, P-792, J-387, F-614

page 25: **Riddle 21**

*micro-chips*

O-512, C-455, B-613, A-334, P-520, M-328, I-403, H-315, L-627, S-351, R-537, N-416

page 26 **riddle 22**

*false teeth*

T-623, U-810, R-562, F-444, N-703, L-911, A-375, B-532, E-655, I-827, H-336, S-788

page 27: **Riddle 23**

*Clock Kent*

R-835, D-643, K-754, W-492, E-633, C-920, N-466, L-311, U-507, O-978, T-782, S-821

page 28: **Riddle 24**

*It was too tweet.*

O-645, M-852, I-787, A-430, P-761, T-923, E-558, H-246, L-332, S-624, R-815, W-476

page 29: **Riddle 25**

*the duck-tor*

U-533, Y-620, T-491, B-765, N-840, K-924, H-375, R-758, O-912, C-286, D-547, E-685

page 30: **Riddle 26**

*frosted flakes*

P-16, F-12, A-15, K-9, S-18, D-6, O-11, L-10, R-17, T-14, H-8, E-7

page 31: **Riddle 27**

*It was in a jam.*

W-5, J-63, I-32, E-76, L-16, S-41, R-28, A-50, O-84, M-68, T-56, N-37

page 32: **Riddle 28**

*a laundro-mutt*

U-12, M-13, A-20, E-36, D-53, V-40, L-51, N-22, O-46, R-35, B-21, T-34

page 33 **riddle 29**

*ice hoppy*

P-84, I-33, N-11, D-27, O-20, A-39, H-18, Y-75, S-63, C-52, E-36, R-45

page 34: **Riddle 30**

*It heard a hiss.*

A-74, V-32, H-83, L-25, E-36, B-20, T-61, R-47, I-18, D-52, O-49, S-56

page 35: **Riddle 31**

*with sonic brooms*

B-42, W-5, I-26, T-13, C-46, O-50, N-61, M-54, R-75, K-1, S-35, H-16

page 36 **Riddle 32**

*to get a pen for its ink*

E-54, F-15, T-34, P-41, K-38, O-22, G-27, N-66, R-50, S-17, I-75, A-43

page 37: **Riddle 33**

*an eye wet-ness*

Y-16, W-3, F-58, N-17, U-33, P-26, O-48, S-75, E-24, A-62, T-9, L-46

page 38: **Riddle 34**

*Drop them a line.*

O-29, A-18, D-56, N-32, E-14, P-47, I-61, H-24, M-35, R-73, L-69, T-28

page 39: **Riddle 35**

*Take it to a horror movie.*

O-12, D-28, A-15, R-46, I-39, K-58, M-47, T-9, B-32, E-74, V-54, H-63

page 40: **Riddle 36**

*to get to the other pride*

E-303, P-192, R-446, T-157, A-278, L-742, N-211, G-834, O-636, D-405, I-580, H-369

page 41: **Riddle 37**

*a florist fire*

E-222, T-331, O-456, A-304, I-463, N-282, F-512, C-203, L-440, P-545, R-300, S-562

page 42: **Riddle 38**

*to catch her breath*

A-503, B-311, Y-434, O-842, L-520, H-268, E-159, T-683, D-275, R-458, C-107, I-726

page 43: **Riddle 39**

*his trans-parents*

N-641, P-136, H-545, T-352, W-268, R-413, F-193, I-381, E-736, S-554, M-221, A-760

page 44: **Riddle 40**

*No, he prince.*

O-369, R-170, T-317, H-193, A-423, P-162, N-153, E-291, W-388, C-151, I-425, D-328

page 45: **Riddle 41**

*palm trees*

C-250, M-706, K-372, B-423, R-638, T-817, E-149, A-580, S-268, P-415, L-161, F-564

page 46: **Riddle 42**

*battle-sheep*

L-806, N-324, H-171, R-549, B-438, U-270, S-189, A-767, C-318, T-652, P-207, E-563

page 47: **Riddle 43**

*What a re-leaf!*

H-718, L-375, E-339, Y-103, W-657, N-469, S-442, A-126, C-175, F-888, T-277, R-244

page 48: **Riddle 44**

*the lights witch*

S-337, I-509, T-222, C-528, A-241, H-197, E-143, K-766, R-474, L-758, G-642, W-185

page 49 **Riddle 45**

*Hi honey, I'm hair.*

O-398, N-263, E-185, L-474, D-256, Y-647, I-739, A-498, H-532, M-159, R-326, U-565

page 50: **Riddle 46**

*Gee, I'm stumped.*

M-289, R-456, U-569, A-127, I-645, D-753, P-566, G-748, N-187, S-372, T-458, E-275

page 51: **Riddle 47**

*a chicken*

K-393, T-574, E-465, H-287, R-656, A-153, S-745, C-228, M-677, D-362, I-523, N-436

page 52: **Riddle 48**

*people bumps*

B-732, A-187, U-368, R-418, M-166, O-343, F-679, E-248, P-467, L-228, S-574, G-758

page 53: **Riddle 49**

*finger tips*

E-339, F-175, A-223, L-611, P-208, I-612, T-764, N-556, B-434, G-573, S-349, R-107

page 54: **Riddle 50**

*I'm all ears.*

M-11, I-5, D-15, L-8, C-9, F-13, R-17, J-16, A-14, N-10, S-18, E-12

page 55: **Riddle 51**

*I glove you.*

L-48, C-22, V-11, N-25, A-41, E-54, I-39, O-7, U-67, G-56, Y-5, R-34

page 56: **Riddle 52**

*a bouy-ant*

U-89, E-9, N-53, B-67, G-16, O-31, A-70, R-92, S-7, Y-28, H-82, T-44

page 57: **Riddle 53**

*the can opener*

A-36, R-17, H-45, L-69, C-53, O-11, T-86, P-52, N-97, D-40, S-74, E-88

page 58: **Riddle 54**

*the turtle*

T-699, L-543, U-226, F-130, A-971, E-203, K-568, N-785, R-356, O-547, H-854, D-482

page 59: **Riddle 55**

*a mess-terpiece*

E-228, P-189, N-945, A-367, C-472, R-810, M-571, O-739, K-797, T-804, I-658, S-463

page 60: **Riddle 56**

*hide and shriek*

F-311, E-155, S-262, T-804, I-520, N-927, A-689, H-736, K-478, D-864, R-97, M-243

page 61: **Riddle 57**

*Men! Get in the boat!*

E-645, H-158, N-787, A-380, G-761, L-285, I-157, T-168, B-332, D-624, O-553, M-476